STUDY GUIDE

LIVING

AT THE

NEXT

LEADERS EDITION

LEVEL

Published by AVAIL

For foreign and subsidiary rights, contact the author.

Cover design by: Joe DeLeon

ISBN: 978-1-950718-91-7   1 2 3 4 5 6 7 8 9 10

Printed in the United States of America

STUDY GUIDE

LIVING

AT THE

NEXT

LEADERS EDITION

LEVEL

COURTNEY MCBATH

AVAIL

CONTENTS

PART 1: THE NEXT LEVEL JOURNEY

Chapter 1. What Is Living at the Next Level?..........................8

Chapter 2. A Friendship Journey:
What We Were Made For 16

PART 2: LIMITATIONS AT THE NEXT LEVEL

Chapter 3. When the Friendship Journey
Takes an Unexpected Turn................................. 26

Chapter 4. Stamina in Limitations... 34

Chapter 5. Your Designer Prison 42

PART 3: BREAKING OUT AT THE NEXT LEVEL

Chapter 6. Who Turned On the Light? 52

Chapter 7. Get Up Quickly... 60

Chapter 8. Get Dressed.. 68

PART 4: MOVING FORWARD AT THE NEXT LEVEL

Chapter 9. Walking Out 78

Chapter 10. Courage to Walk On 86

PART 1:

The Next Level Journey

chapter 1

What Is Living at the Next Level?

"Friendship with God is the Next Level. Once we 'get there,' then the journey of life in God with all of its ups and downs begins. The ups and downs don't make us any less 'there.'"

READING TIME

Read Chapter 1: "What Is Living at the Next Level?," in *What Is Living At the Next Level?*, reflect on the questions and discuss your answers with your study group.

What experience from your childhood, or even later life, do you remember that you waited, and waited, and waited for? Did it turn out how you'd expected? How or how did it not?

_____

_____

_____

_____

_____

_____

_____

What have been and are your dreams? Which have come to fruition?

_____

_____

_____

_____

_____

REFLECT ON

Exodus 33:11:

"Thus the LORD used to speak to Moses face to face, just as a man speaks to his friend."

What frustrations and obstacles do you continue to face as you pursue the dreams that have eluded you?

_____

_____

_____

_____

_____

_____

Do you agree with the following statement? *As God's friends, we, too, are living in the place of promise.* Why or why not?

_____

_____

_____

_____

_____

_____

Which of the three responses to frustration most match your style of dealing with it? How does it manifest?

1. You give up on your dreams.
2. You grit your teeth, swallow your pain, and maintain your "waiting to arrive" posture.
3. You learn to fully experience your journey with God right now.

_____

_____

_____

_____

_____

_____

How could embracing the idea that you are currently living in a place of promise change your outlook on life? What habits would you have to change?

_____

_____

_____

_____

_____

_____

What do you "do" to cultivate your heart for friendship with God? How is it working for you?

_____

_____

_____

_____

_____

_____

When have you become so fixated on a dream or future event that you failed to recognize the blessings you had already received?

_____

_____

_____

_____

_____

_____

What do you value in your earthly friendships that are guaranteed in friendship with God? What does friendship with God offer that earthly friendship can't?

_____

_____

_____

_____

_____

_____

What causes you to struggle to believe that God can use you to lead at higher levels?

_____

_____

_____

_____

_____

_____

chapter 2

A Friendship Journey: What We Were Made For

"The moment you open your heart to receive Christ, you enter a friendship with God and begin your Next Level journey."

READING TIME

Read Chapter 2: "A Friendship Journey: What We Were Made For," in *What Is Living At the Next Level?*, reflect on the questions and discuss your answers with your study group.

What do you remember of the moment you opened your heart to receive Christ? What kind of initiation did you receive both in the heavenly realm and on earth?

_____

_____

_____

_____

_____

_____

What does the paradox that friendship with God is the starting point, the gateway to the Next Level, and the destination reveal to you?

_____

_____

_____

_____

_____

_____

REFLECT ON

Revelation 4:11 (KJV)

"Thou art worthy, O Lord, to receive glory and honour and power: for thou hast created all things, and for thy pleasure they are and were created."

What is your experience with God pursuing people to be His friends?

_____

_____

_____

_____

_____

_____

_____

Do you agree with the following statement? *God doesn't extend His friendship just to keep us out of hell. Jesus came so that we could live in friendship with God and walk closely with Him on earth.* Why or why not?

_____

_____

_____

_____

_____

_____

_____

When, in your leadership journey, do you still feel very alone, despite the fact that you have ministry partners?

_____

_____

_____

_____

_____

_____

My little children, I am writing these things to you so that you may not sin. And if anyone sins, we have an Advocate with the Father, Jesus Christ the righteous.
—1 John 2:1

What do you see are the challenges of pleasing God by loving Him, by walking closely with Him, as we were made to do?

_____

_____

_____

_____

_____

_____

What opposition do you face—spiritual or physical—in your walk? What is your traditional way of dealing with it?

_____

_____

_____

_____

_____

_____

How would you counsel a person experiencing trouble if he or she doesn't know from whom or where it's coming?

_____

_____

_____

_____

_____

To what extent have you allowed yourself to be "at peace" with the Father, since you've been justified by faith?

_____

_____

_____

_____

_____

Considering that you are called to bear the burdens of those you lead, how consistently are you allowing your Friend and Heavenly Father to refresh and renew you?

_____

_____

_____

_____

_____

PART 2:

Limitations at the Next Level

chapter 3

When the Friendship Journey Takes an Unexpected Turn

"When our journey in friendship with God seems to lead us to prison, we have to process our way through a storm of emotions. 'What happened?' we want to know."

READING TIME

Read Chapter 3: "When the Friendship Journey Takes an Unexpected Turn," in *What Is Living At the Next Level?*, reflect on the questions and discuss your answers with your study group.

When have you experienced an astounding period of growth only to be followed by a period of resistance or stagnation in your leadership role?

_____

_____

_____

_____

_____

_____

When have you felt that your journey of friendship with God seemed to lead you into prison? What were your thoughts, feelings, spoken words?

_____

_____

_____

_____

_____

REFLECT ON

1 Thessalonians 5:16-18

"Rejoice always; pray without ceasing; in everything give thanks; for this is God's will for you in Christ Jesus."

How would you encourage someone else who believed that his or her friendship with God led to hardship?

_____

_____

_____

_____

_____

Do you agree with the following statement? *If we've landed in a prison, then God knows why and has plans to work our incarceration out for our good. He is keeping us on the path of life, even when it feels like we've been hurled headlong into a ditch.* Why or why not?

_____

_____

_____

_____

_____

Jesus promised His disciples in John 16:33, "In this world, you will have trouble." Consider the three areas in which people are "limited" in their walks with God. Reflect on each of the different types you've experienced.

1. Limits you can't control
2. Limitations that result from your own actions or decisions
3. Limitations that result from life happening

_____

_____

_____

_____

_____

How have you seen God "utilize the cards you've been dealt" for His redemptive purposes?

_____

_____

_____

_____

_____

_____

How do you balance the reality of the consequences of your or other people's sin with God's desire to bring relief to the pain?

_____

_____

_____

_____

_____

Does your leadership strategy lean more toward preventing difficult situations or determining responsibility for them? When have you been unable to accomplish either of those tasks?

_____

_____

_____

_____

_____

_____

What are your greatest challenges when it comes to trusting God to mend your heart, redeem your confines, and help you live in peace as long as those limitations last?

_____

_____

_____

_____

_____

_____

What are your thoughts regarding cultivating a heart of gratitude to God during these times? How can thankfulness, prayer, and forgiveness help one intentionally do this?

_____

_____

_____

_____

_____

Stamina in Limitations

"Why, at certain times in life, does it seem like drama, struggle, and crisis mass-produce?"

READING TIME

Read Chapter 4: "Stamina in Limitations," in *What Is Living At the Next Level?*, reflect on the questions and discuss your answers with your study group.

What is your experience with perseverance? Does the possibility that others are watching influence your determination?

_____

_____

_____

_____

_____

_____

When has someone else had greater insight about your struggles than you've had? How did that person communicate that insight to you? What was your response?

_____

_____

_____

_____

_____

REFLECT ON

Isaiah 40:31 (KJV)

"But they that wait upon the LORD shall renew their strength; they shall mount up with wings as eagles; they shall run, and not be weary; and they shall walk, and not faint."

Do you agree with the following statement? *Half the battle against frustration is seeing things differently—it's probably more than half the battle. The way we see things can make or break our ability to endure and directly influence our destiny.* Why or why not?

_____

_____

_____

_____

_____

As God's friends, how—at this moment—do you see that you and the people you lead are living at the Next Level? How do you communicate it so others can share the experience?

_____

_____

_____

_____

_____

_____

How would you encourage someone struggling to transform his or her frustrations, take hold of peace, and build stamina for the rest of the jail term? Use your own ideas or focus on the ones below:

1. Worship
2. "Forget" the past
3. Make plans

_____

_____

_____

_____

_____

_____

What role does your seeking rest play in developing a Next Level heart attitude? What comfort do you take in knowing that ultimately "God must take care of the rest, literally"?

_____

_____

_____

_____

_____

What plans could you make or steps can you take right now that would ease your frustration and renew your hope regarding your limitations?

_____

_____

_____

_____

_____

How would you encourage someone who bailed, regretted it, and is now haunted by his or her decision?

_____

_____

_____

_____

_____

When might it be appropriate to bail? How can you as a leader support a person in this position?

_____

_____

_____

_____

_____

_____

If all is well in the midst of your journey but you still yearn for a life with no limits, is there any area in which you could increase your strength or staying power?

_____

_____

_____

_____

_____

chapter 5

Your Designer Prison

"You may have landed in limitations for any number of reasons, but right there in your cell, God is preserving you, fixing you, building you, and using your limitations to prepare you for the coming phases of your journey."

READING TIME

Read Chapter 5: "Your Designer Prison," in *What Is Living At the Next Level?*, reflect on the questions and discuss your answers with your study group.

When have you felt like you were in the belly of Jonah's fish, only to find out later that it was acting as your life preserver? How would you encourage someone you think is in the very same place but doesn't see it that way?

_____

_____

_____

_____

_____

Why is it often difficult to believe your or someone else's "prison" could have a good purpose?

_____

_____

_____

_____

_____

REFLECT ON

Psalm 139:7-10

"Where can I go from Your Spirit? Or where can I flee from Your presence? If I ascend to heaven, You are there; If I make my bed in Sheol, behold, You are there. If I take the wings of the dawn, if I dwell in the remotest part of the sea, even there Your hand will lead me, and Your right hand will lay hold of me."

In what situation can you see God putting limits on a person for his or her own good?

_____

_____

_____

_____

_____

_____

_____

Identify some of the ways that God is reaching out to you, using your losses and limitations to build your friendship with Him.

_____

_____

_____

_____

_____

_____

_____

How would you reassure someone who is wavering in his or her determination that the devil is under God's authority and that when God says, "Enough!" the devil must go?

_____

_____

_____

_____

_____

_____

Do you agree with this statement? *What I love about God is that He doesn't need good materials to make good stuff; He can take intrinsically bad or limiting materials and make them good.* Why or why not?

_____

_____

_____

_____

_____

_____

_____

_____

_____

_____

Which of your weaknesses are becoming clearer to you under the pressure of limitations? In what areas of your character can you feel yourself changing and growing?

_____

_____

_____

_____

_____

_____

_____

_____

_____

_____

If prison can be a liberating phase of the journey where God grows you, loves you, and applies His healing balm of grace to you, how can you implement the following strategies to maximize your contentment through it?

1. Come Out of Denial
2. Make a Decision
3. Welcome Delayed Gratification
4. Believe in the Power of God's Plans

_____

_____

_____

_____

_____

In your leadership role, when have you seen someone settle for just the experience of internal change in his or her heart, mind, or character while relinquishing hope of seeing things change externally?

_____

_____

_____

_____

_____

What scriptures do you recommend to someone who needs to understand what God's Word says so he or she can come into agreement with it in preparation for release?

_____

_____

_____

_____

_____

PART 3:

Breaking Out at the Next Level

Who Turned On the Light?

"Everything pertaining to us must showcase God's love, point the world in God's direction, and produce worship of Him. If you are experiencing a limitation in your life, then, ultimately, God will use it somehow to bring Himself glory."

READING TIME

Read Chapter 6: "Who Turned On the Light?," in *What Is Living At the Next Level?*, reflect on the questions, and discuss your answers with your study group.

What situation in your life didn't work out according to plan, but you trusted God in the midst of the loss and disappointment, and He was glorified in it?

_____

_____

_____

_____

_____

What encouragement can you offer to someone who doesn't believe yet that God is efficient? He gets maximum work out of our limitations, and then He moves us on: the prison sentence is over.

_____

_____

_____

_____

_____

REFLECT ON

Hebrews 10:23

"Let us hold fast the confession of our hope without wavering, for He who promised is faithful."

What situation has caused you to "raise the bar" in what you expect from God? How has He, Himself, challenged you to embrace a heart of expectancy toward God?

_____

_____

_____

_____

_____

_____

What are the hazards of having low expectations of God?

_____

_____

_____

_____

_____

Do you agree with the following statement? *Your situation may not appear critical to you, but some of the things you've been praying about, hoping for, and expecting from God are all connected to a decision you've got to make right now about responding to the light. When God turns on the light, you can't sleep on it. You can't play with it. You've got to wake up.* Why or why not?

_____

_____

_____

_____

_____

_____

SHARE YOUR STORY

Therefore I say to you, all things for which you pray and ask, believe that you have received them, and they will be granted you. —Mark 11:24

What could cause a person's faith to "keep sleeping" through the wake-up call or to grasp the covers more tightly and hope for five more minutes?

_____

_____

_____

_____

_____

_____

In what areas do you need to become more expectant toward God? How do you plan to go about it? Who can you ask to help you if you feel like your faith is not strong enough for the task?

_____

_____

_____

_____

_____

If it is by engaging with His Word that we learn to hear God's voice and understand His heart, how can you encourage those you lead to do more than just read or hear it?

_____

_____

_____

_____

_____

_____

How can you be a leader who constantly turns on the light of the Word, so it can penetrate deep into people's prisons?

_____

_____

_____

_____

_____

In what area are you ready to become expectant again?

_____

_____

_____

_____

_____

Get Up Quickly

*"The truth is we really don't know
what's best for us all the time."*

READING TIME

Read Chapter 7: "Get Up Quickly," in *What Is Living At the Next Level?*, reflect on the questions, and discuss your answers with your study group.

What in your life at one time appeared to be a blessing, but quickly became a curse because you were not able to handle it properly?

_____

_____

_____

_____

_____

_____

What has God withheld from you in which the withholding turned out to be a blessing?

_____

_____

_____

_____

_____

_____

REFLECT ON

Deuteronomy 4:29

"But from there you will seek the LORD your God, and you will find Him if you search for Him with all your heart and all your soul."

As a leader, when have you had to carefully follow God's instructions, even when they haven't made sense? How do you influence your people to do the same?

_____

_____

_____

_____

_____

_____

Do you agree with the following statement? *While God moved supernaturally to ensure Peter's rescue, He also required Peter to do a couple of things—to take responsibility and do his part.* Why or why not?

_____

_____

_____

_____

_____

_____

How does one's "seeing" and "responding" when God performs the release miracle indicate that the needed internal changes in a person's heart will continue to work themselves out as a heart to seek God?

_____

_____

_____

_____

_____

_____

And behold, an angel of the Lord suddenly appeared and a light shone in the cell; and he struck Peter's

What do you think the Bible means when it says that as a man "thinks in his heart, so is he" (Proverbs 23:7)? How does it apply to living at the Next Level?

_____

_____

_____

_____

_____

Do you, as a leader, tend to focus more on your own internal or external changes? Why do think that is? Which would you prefer to see in the people you lead?

_____

_____

_____

_____

What peace can an insecure person find in the fact that if he or she will just say "yes," then God will get him or her up Himself? How has God made allowances for that in that He can handle it when a person pleads, "Help my unbelief!"

_____

_____

_____

_____

How has your leadership journey challenged you to move in what seems to be an impossible direction quickly?

_____

_____

_____

_____

_____

_____

In what areas do you sense a need to increase your agility, so you can move even more quickly if the situation calls for it?

_____

_____

_____

_____

_____

Get Dressed

"If you are going to take a journey anywhere, then you must take time to get ready. We [have] to get ready, or the trip could prove chaotic, stressful, and unproductive."

READING TIME

Read Chapter 8: "Get Dressed," in *What Is Living At the Next Level?*, reflect on the questions and discuss your answers with your study group.

What would you say to someone who believes that time spent preparing is time wasted that could be spent journeying?

_____

_____

_____

_____

_____

_____

What are your greatest challenges when it comes to obeying God? How would you encourage someone struggling with the same challenges or their own?

_____

_____

_____

_____

_____

REFLECT ON

Jeremiah 7:23

"But this is what I commanded them, saying, 'Obey My voice, and I will be your God, and you will be My people; and you will walk in all the way which I command you, that it may be well with you.'"

Do you agree with the following statement? *If I know God's commands come to indicate growth, prepare me for the future, and work for my good—and I know this because the commands are coming from my Friend—then I become energized to put my faith in action and obey Him.* Why or why not?

_____

_____

_____

_____

_____

_____

Many people coming out of prison are unprepared to make their own choices, since their time in lock-up—almost every minute and action—was controlled by someone else. What habits learned during your incarceration in your designer prison can you implement wholeheartedly—not just fall back on—on your continued journey with God?

_____

_____

_____

_____

_____

What areas of your leadership are you still unsure you'll be able to "put on"? If you don't have any, how would you encourage another leader who does?

_____

_____

_____

_____

_____

As you're reminded of where you've been by the "dirt" on your sandals, how can you appreciate what the dirt signifies?

_____

_____

_____

_____

_____

How does a leader's preparation benefit the people that he or she leads? How might that thought make it easier to endure the time of preparation when a person really just wants to get on with the journey?

_____

_____

_____

_____

_____

What has God given you that other people need? What are you doing to share it with them?

_____

_____

_____

_____

_____

What definitive steps should you prepare to take in this season of your leadership growth?

_____

_____

_____

_____

_____

_____

Who can you ask to hold you accountable as you endeavor to take those steps?

_____

_____

_____

_____

_____

_____

PART 4:

Moving Forward at the Next Level

Walking Out

"You are empowered by God for this moment! You have all that you need. Everything required of you can be found in your friendship with God."

Read Chapter 9: "Walking Out," in *What Is Living At the Next Level?*, reflect on the questions and discuss your answers with your study group.

How has your time in prison changed your perception of yourself and your role as leader?

_____

_____

_____

_____

_____

_____

What's the difference between the optimism that comes from truly believing that God has changed you during your time in prison as opposed to wishful thinking or bravado?

_____

_____

_____

_____

_____

REFLECT ON

Proverbs 3:5-6

"Trust in the Lord with all your heart and do not lean on your own understanding. In all your ways acknowledge Him, and He will make your paths straight."

Do you agree with the following statement? *As you wait for God's guidance on your way out of prison, you do so serving Him, doing whatever He asks, and anticipating His desires. This is faith-waiting—and it will be fulfilled.* Why or why not?

_____

_____

_____

_____

_____

Fears may arise because you can't see where you're going or you don't know the way. Perhaps visions of the past—bad decisions, relationship changes, or personal setbacks—prevent your walking past your "guards." What is your strategy for overcoming these obstacles?

_____

_____

_____

_____

_____

_____

What role does "asking" take as a person deepens his or her commitment to developing a heart to seek God? What might prevent a person from continuing to ask God for anything necessary for the journey?

_____

_____

_____

_____

_____

_____

Where or from whom do you seek God's guidance? What specifically do you feel you are going to need guidance for on this next stage of your leadership journey?

_____

_____

_____

_____

_____

How would you encourage another leader who feels that he or she has no right to another chance? What about one who lacked support from others or has accepted defeat as the norm in the past?

_____

_____

_____

_____

_____

Where will your faith and diligence need to be applied in order to get into the "city of your greater influence"?

_____

_____

_____

_____

_____

What would you say to someone who is physically free, but whose mind is still very much imprisoned?

_____

_____

_____

_____

_____

_____

How will you embrace this new season of freedom? How will you exercise your faith and go through the gates to your city phase?

_____

_____

_____

_____

_____

_____

chapter 10

Courage to Walk On

"There are seasons in our lives when God walks so closely with us, when His Word becomes so real to us, that we feel almost the way Peter must have felt in the presence of the angel—as if we are being led step by step; as if our steps literally are being "ordered" by God ... Then we reach a point where things seem to shift; the angel leaves us and we have to go on."

Who can you think of in the Bible who could have been very afraid when his or her leader had gone on? What was that person's response? How did his or her situation unfold?

_____

_____

_____

_____

_____

How can a person keep at bay the feeling of being alone or abandoned by his or her heavenly guide now that that particular presence has taken a different turn at the crossroads?

_____

_____

_____

_____

What challenges do you face when it comes to connecting with others—leaders or lay people?

_____

_____

_____

_____

_____

_____

_____

Do you agree with the following statement? *When we become God's friends, we become part of "His family (John 1:12)." We are inextricably tied to others.* Why or why not?

_____

_____

_____

_____

_____

_____

_____

Think of the "stars" in the first movie you made. Who were they? Why did you cast them in those roles? How will the "stars" in your current movie be different?

_____

_____

_____

_____

_____

_____

Who are your Rhodas? How do those people fulfill that role for you? How will you communicate your needs as a leader, so they can more effectively pray for you and lift you up?

_____

_____

_____

_____

_____

_____

_____

_____

_____

_____

For whom can you be a Rhoda? What is your plan for filling that role for others?

_____

_____

_____

_____

_____

_____

_____

_____

_____

_____

_____

_____

What did you empty yourself of while you were imprisoned that you now see left a space that needs to be filled? How will cultivating the four heart attitudes fill your empty spaces in a way that brings God glory and causes you to thrive in life at the Next Level?

1. A heart for friendship with God
2. A heart of gratitude to God
3. A heart of expectancy toward God
4. A heart to seek God

_____

_____

_____

_____

_____

_____

_____

How have the above heart attitudes given you courage and a greater measure of faith to live at the Next Level?

_____

_____

_____

_____

_____

What opportunities do you see for more effective leadership now that you have passed certain barriers and are on to the next phase of your journey?

_____

_____

_____

_____

_____